Windy and the fluff flowers

written by Tia Batten

Illustrated by Monika Marzec

Windy, the wind gust, was **angry**.

She wanted to stay up high in the sky and blow the puffy clouds all around,

but she wasn't allowed to today.

She was **grounded.**

So instead of blowing soft, fluffy clouds across the blue skies, she was sent down, low to the ground.

Drifting along the prickly, brown grass and bare trees was boring, Windy thought.

Until she came across the fluffiest, softest, most cloud-like plant she'd ever seen!

Windy breezed her way towards the fluffy flower. She was so excited that she let out a huge gust.

Oh no!!

The beautiful flower burst into little bits of fluff that swirled and twirled all around, floating away from Windy.

She chased after them, but every time she came close, the fluff just blew further and further away.

No matter how hard she tried, Windy wasn't able to catch a single fluff.

She drifted back up into the sky and looked down at all the fluffs that had found a place to rest among the dried grass.

Disappointed, Windy decided she would come back tomorrow to try and catch one.

When Windy sailed back to the ground, she couldn't find a single fluff.

Windy was sad.

Her fluff friends had all disappeared.
She puffed out a goodbye and billowed back up
into the sky to return to her cloud duties.

When she returned a few days later, she was shocked to see bright yellow flowers in the exact same spots where the fluffs had rested.

Windy fluttered from flower to flower, admiring their happy color and soft petals.

They weren't the same as her fluff flower, but these bright flowers certainly helped to cheer her up.

Windy returned, day after day, to visit her yellow friends. She saw butterflies and bees coming to visit them too.

They would gather nectar and pollen, then buzz or flutter away.

But one morning, she drifted down to find all of her flowers had closed up.

"No, no, no!"

She zipped from flower to flower, hoping to see one with bright yellow petals, but every single one was shut tight.

Windy didn't know what could have hurt her yellow friends. She must have done something wrong.

She was so sad that she stormed into the clouds and stayed up there for days, until she was sent down once again. Reluctantly, she drifted in the direction of her old flower friends.

Windy was surprised! When she arrived, in the place of her bright yellow flowers, she found fluffy cloud flowers!

She twirled with joy, and the plants around her fluttered in the wake.

She watched as a few puffs of fluff drifted away.

As gently as she could, Windy floated towards one of the fluff flowers.

She huffed in surprise when she saw that at the bottom of the fluff was a tiny seed.

That's when she realized that when she had blown the first fluffs away, the seeds must have fallen onto the ground and grown into her pretty yellow flowers, and those yellow flowers had become these fluffy clouds flowers.

She had helped the flowers, not hurt them.
Windy felt **proud**.

Windy moved to the center of the field where the fluffy cloud flowers stood, then she twirled and let out a big burst of air.

Windy followed as many as she could, happily blowing them along her gentle breeze until the fluffs found the perfect place to rest.

A few days later, when Windy soared up above the field, she saw hundreds and hundreds of yellow flowers. She whirled with glee. She had succeeded!

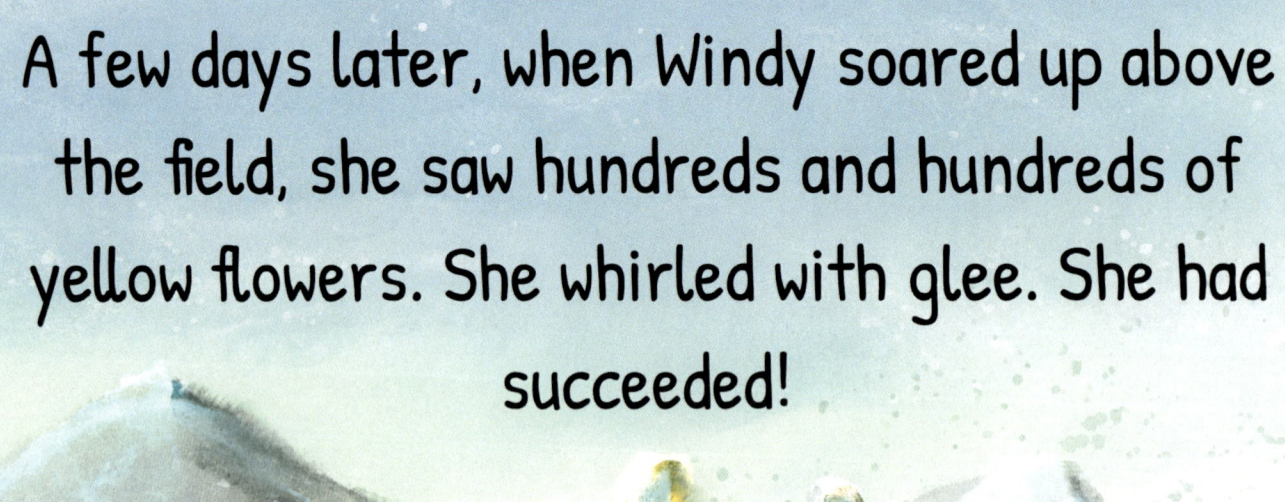

From that day on,
Windy took care of her flowers,
blowing the fluff to make sure they
would grow all over,
bringing life and color
to the once empty field.

Read Tia's other book

For Nick, Lyle, Nellie, Bear, and Jamie.

Copyright © 2024 Tia Batten.
All rights reserved.

Made in the USA
Monee, IL
07 January 2025